MAJOR DISASTERS

2022 PAKISTAN FLOODS

BY TRUDY BECKER

WWW.APEXEDITIONS.COM

Apex is distributed by North Star Editions:
sales@northstareditions.com | 888-417-0195

Produced for Apex by Red Line Editorial.

Photographs ©: Fareed Khan/AP Images, cover; Shutterstock Images, 1, 4–5, 6–7, 9, 10–11, 13, 14–15, 18, 19, 22–23, 26–27, 29; iStockphoto, 8, 12, 20–21, 24; Zahid Hussain/AP Images, 16–17

Library of Congress Control Number: 2023910183

ISBN
978-1-63738-754-2 (hardcover)
978-1-63738-797-9 (paperback)
978-1-63738-880-8 (ebook pdf)
978-1-63738-840-2 (hosted ebook)

Printed in the United States of America
Mankato, MN
012024

NOTE TO PARENTS AND EDUCATORS

Apex books are designed to build literacy skills in striving readers. Exciting, high-interest content attracts and holds readers' attention. The text is carefully leveled to allow students to achieve success quickly. Additional features, such as bolded glossary words for difficult terms, help build comprehension.

TABLE OF CONTENTS

CHAPTER 1
ENDLESS RAIN 4

CHAPTER 2
FLOODING DISASTER 10

CHAPTER 3
MASSIVE DAMAGE 16

CHAPTER 4
WORK TO RECOVER 22

COMPREHENSION QUESTIONS • 28
GLOSSARY • 30
TO LEARN MORE • 31
ABOUT THE AUTHOR • 31
INDEX • 32

It's 2022. **Monsoon** season arrives in Pakistan. Heavy rain pours down. The Indus River starts to overflow. Water rushes along the ground.

Some monsoons blow wet air over an area. This change brings heavy rain.

Soon, water covers roads and fields. It fills houses. Days and weeks pass, but the rain doesn't stop. Monsoon season continues. More and more areas flood.

MONSOON SEASON

In Pakistan, monsoon season happens from late spring to late summer. The rain can be welcome during hot weather. But too much rain can cause disasters.

In the city of Karachi, Pakistan, streets filled with water.

FAST FACT

Some people took boats or swam to travel through flooded areas.

People hurry to escape the rising water. Their homes are destroyed. They swim through muddy water to reach higher ground.

When an area floods, people evacuate. They try to go somewhere safe.

The 2022 floods damaged more than two million buildings throughout Pakistan.

CHAPTER 2

FLOODING DISASTER

A series of huge floods hit Pakistan in 2022. From June to August, three times more monsoon rain than normal poured down.

The 2022 floods were some of Pakistan's worst flooding in years.

FAST FACT

Parts of Pakistan got 15 inches (38 cm) of rain per day.

Rivers and streams throughout Pakistan filled with water and overflowed.

The extra water had nowhere to go. It caused flash floods. Water filled buildings and fields. The standing water stayed for months.

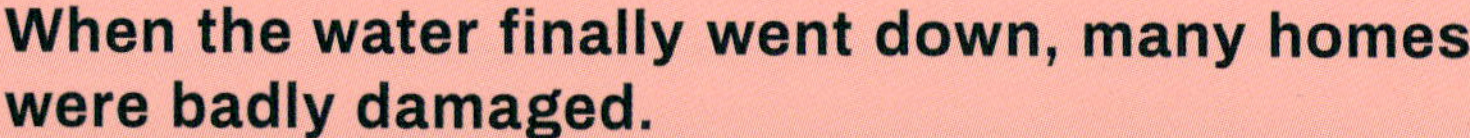

When the water finally went down, many homes were badly damaged.

Climate change played a part in the floods. Hot weather made the air wetter. That led to extra rain. Melting **glaciers** also added water to the Indus River.

The 2010 floods were also caused by climate change. More than 1,000 people died in the floods.

CLIMATE DISASTERS

Climate change has led to other disasters in Pakistan. In 2010, the country had bad flooding. In 2015, there was a strong **heat wave**. Both events killed many people.

CHAPTER 3

MASSIVE DAMAGE

The results of the floods were terrible. Around 2,000 people died. And tens of thousands lost their homes.

At one point, one-third of land in Pakistan was underwater.

Water completely covered some villages. Other villages turned into islands. Some people became stranded. Many lost access to clean water. As a result, they often became sick or died.

Swimming or walking through dirty water can make people sick.

Mosquitoes lay eggs in water. They spread malaria and other diseases.

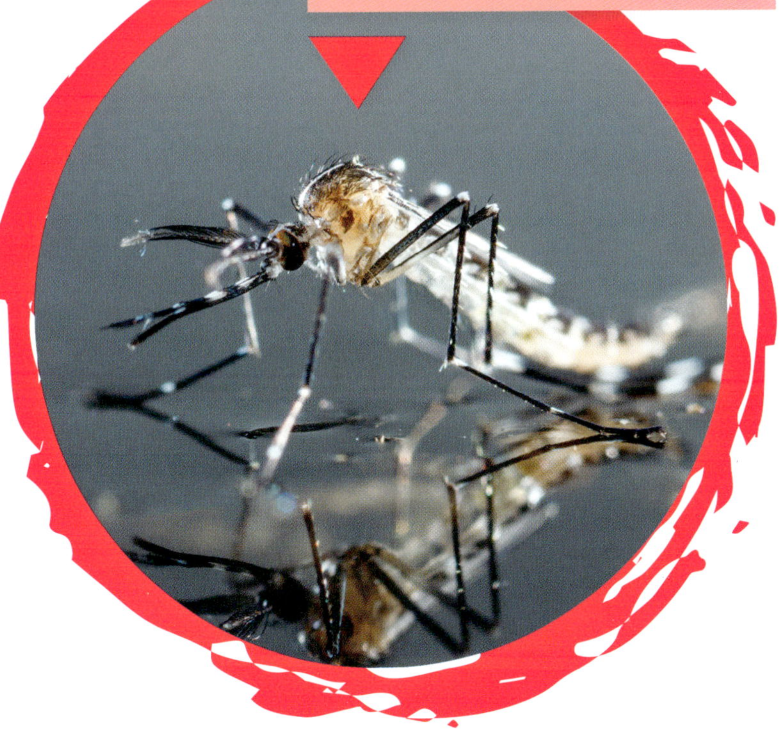

WATER PROBLEMS

Dirty water can spread disease. People may get sick if they drink or touch it. In some flooded buildings, dampness causes mold to grow. Mold can also make people sick.

Across the country, farms were covered in water. Crops could not grow. People lost their sources of food and **income**. Many schools were destroyed as well.

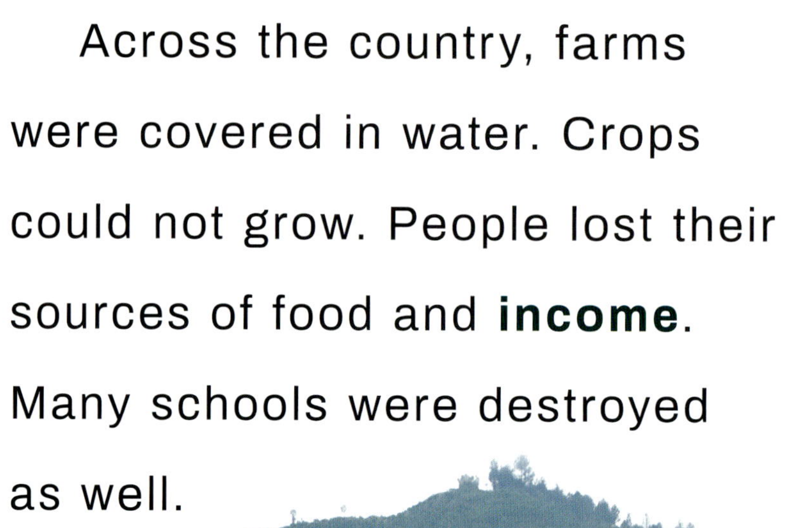

The damage to homes, buildings, and farms caused more than $10 billion of loss.

FAST FACT
The Indus River turned into a giant lake during Pakistan's 2022 floods.

CHAPTER 4

WORK TO RECOVER

After the floods, people around the world sent aid. Many gave food, clothes, and clean water. Others donated money.

Many people lost everything in the floods. They stayed in tents at camps.

Helpers tried to find new homes for people. They also worked to rebuild. However, many roads and bridges had collapsed. That made it harder to send help.

In many places, floodwater washed away parts of the ground.

Many cities in Pakistan have trouble draining water quickly enough to prevent flooding.

Scientists are studying weather patterns related to climate change. This can help them **predict** future floods. However, getting ready can still be hard.

UNEVEN IMPACTS

Climate change affects Pakistan very strongly. But Pakistan produces very little of the **emissions** that cause it. To avoid future disasters, other countries must make changes.

COMPREHENSION QUESTIONS

Write your answers on a separate piece of paper.

1. Write a few sentences explaining why the 2022 Pakistan floods happened.

2. Do you think it's more important to send aid right away or to work to rebuild? Why?

3. In what other year did Pakistan have bad flooding?

   A. 2000
   B. 2010
   C. 2015

4. How could studying weather help scientists predict floods?

   A. They could tell when more rain might fall.
   B. They could cause more rain to fall.
   C. They could stop tracking temperatures.

5. What does **stranded** mean in this book?

Other villages turned into islands. Some people became ***stranded****.*

A. paid a lot of money to do something
B. sent to a place that is far away
C. stuck in a place that is hard to leave

6. What does **donated** mean in this book?

Many gave food, clothes, and clean water. Others ***donated*** *money.*

A. gave something to people in need
B. took something away from others
C. sent something in the mail

Answer key on page 32.

GLOSSARY

architect

A person who makes plans for buildings.

climate change

A dangerous long-term change in Earth's temperature and weather patterns.

emissions

Gases that are released into the air, especially harmful ones.

glaciers

Large, slow-moving bodies of ice.

heat wave

A period of unusually hot weather.

income

Money people get from working.

monsoon

A strong wind that causes a season of very wet or dry weather in an area.

predict

To guess what will happen in the future.

BOOKS

Dalgleish, Sharon. *Floods*. Mendota Heights, MN: Apex Editions, 2023.

London, Martha. *Floods*. Minneapolis: Abdo Publishing, 2020.

Pettiford, Rebecca. *Floods*. Minneapolis: Bellwether Media, 2020.

ONLINE RESOURCES

Visit **www.apexeditions.com** to find links and resources related to this title.

ABOUT THE AUTHOR

Trudy Becker lives in Minneapolis, Minnesota. She likes exploring new places and loves anything involving books.

INDEX

A
aid, 22

B
boats, 8

C
climate change, 14–15, 26–27

D
deaths, 15, 16, 18
disease, 19

F
flash floods, 12

G
glaciers, 14

H
heat wave, 15

I
Indus River, 4, 14, 21

M
mold, 19
monsoon season, 4, 6–7

R
rain, 4, 6–7, 10, 12, 14
rebuilding, 25

S
sick, 18–19

ANSWER KEY:
1. Answers will vary; 2. Answers will vary; 3. B; 4. A; 5. C; 6. A